SARA JACKLINE

DIET RECIPES 2022: DIETS

HOW TO GET A NEW DIET WHAT IS DIET CULTURE

Diet Recipes 2022: Diets: How To Get A New Diet - What Is Diet Culture

* Diet Recipes

"A this time, while maximum human beings take a seat down without delay right all the way down to consume, we are not relatively privy to how our meals selections have an effect on the planet. We do not recognize that during every Big Mac there's a hint of the tropical rainforests, and with each billion burgers offered some other hundred species end up wiped out. We do not recognize that withinside the sizzle of our steaks there may be the iconic of creatures, the mining of our dirt, the reducing of our woods, the hurting of our economy, and therefore the dissolving of our health. We do not listen withinside the sizzle the decision of the keen tens of thousands and thousands who might also additionally instead be taken care of.

We do not see the toxic pollutants accumulating withinside the developed methods of existence, harming our youths and our earth for a while to return. In any case, while we end up privy to the impact of our meals selections, we are able to by no means definitely forget it. indeed, we are able to push the entirety to the returned of our brains, and that we might also additionally want to try and do this, now and again, to undergo the immensity of what is included.

However, the sector itself will remind us, as will our adolescents, and thusly, the creatures and the woods and the sky and the waterways, that we're an element of this international, and it is a chunk people. Everything is profoundly associated,

at that factor, the alternatives we make in our normal lives have a tremendous effect, on our very own health and imperativeness, but moreover at the lives of various creatures, and surely at the destiny of existence on earth.

Fortunately, we have got triggered to be grateful what is first-rate for us with the aid of using and with the aid of using is moreover first-rate for extraordinary varieties of existence, and for the life emotionally supportive networks on which we as an entire depend."

* How To Diet For A New America

"Significantly pleasurable and moving… the spearheading suit of… Rachel Carson's Silent Spring."

The Washington Post

"In a youthful, now no longer offensive voice, Robbins offers us why an altruistic lifestyle cannot be primarily based totally upon a heartless association of meals creation. Robbins would not play on blame, but offers us how our very own prosperity is hooked up to the event of basically new sensibilities to non-human existence."

Frances Moore Lappe' Author of Diet for a bit Planet

"John Robbins has composed a usually exceptional, convincing ee-e book, one certain to shake our inner most center. Diet For a substitution America is probably an absolute necessity for everybody involved approximately nature, health, and existence."

Las Vegas Sun

"We by no means propose extraordinary books our very own, but we do with Diet For a substitution America. it is it appears that evidently one a number of the preeminent massive reviews of the 20 th century."

Harvey and Marilyn Diamond creators of match Life

"Diet For a substitution America is magnificent! I cannot commend sufficient of it. This ee-e book is probably a discovery withinside the look at of health and a satisfaction to peruse. nobody who endures (or whose pals and own circle of relatives endure) from the maladies inside current reminiscence can undergo to miss this extreme message. for the duration of a fascinating fashion, John Robbins indicates us the first-rate method to make health for ourselves, our adolescents, and thusly the sector we live in bed ."

Dr. John McDougall Author, The McDougall Plan, McDougall's Medicine

"Diet For a substitution America will vitalize the enlivening of America. This easy to peruse the but beautiful ee-e book consists of its region withinside the kitchen, withinside the specialist's office, and in every look at hall, from pre-college to college. For the ones related to organic and policy-pushed troubles, this ee-e book is probably an absolute necessity; so it is for each person who lengthy for possible green gratitude to inspire a normal, moral, and cherishing international."

Laura Huxley, author of This Timeless Moment

"At the factor while our social nutritional propensities are analyzed withinside the unblinking lighting fixtures of empathy and levelheadedness, the propensities ought to and might change. While those propensities will win in lots of human beings, John Robbins' extraordinary ee-e book, which focuses name at a company fashion that those propensities are murdering us in soul and frame, leaves little uncertainty at the inescapable route of our activity."

Slam Dass author Be Here Now, Grist For The Mill

"Diet For a substitution America is probably an crucial asset at the tour in the direction of awareness and sympathy. I like to indicate it with out reservation, and expectation that a first-rate deal of, massive numbers people examine it."

Gary Zukav author The Dancing Wu Li Masters, The Seat of the Soul

"Diet For a substitution America is probably a show-stopper, form of a brand new breath a number of the extraordinary publishings almost about food plan and sustenance. Provocative and invigorating, it is a manner required a tool to be remembered for every health schooling program."

Jack Schwarz President Aletheia Psycho-Physical Foundation

"When constantly kind of a ee-e book indicates up that adjustments the route of an age. Diet For a substitution America is the ee-e book of this decade. Robbins has composed a ee-e book that jewelry with clearness and resolute reality and has an high-quality ability to empower people to require their very very own rate fates. In my more than one lengthy intervals of operating for the authorities help the entirety being identical and for this reason nature, I actually have by no means discovered a ee-e book so ready for affecting change. that is often the ee-e book that we have got been anticipating. Diet For a substitution America is probably a authentic magnum opus."

Bradley Miller Director, Humane Farming Association

"From time to time a ee-e book is going alongside which has the capacity to stir the internal voice of a country. Quiet Spring turned into one such ee-e book; John Robbins' extent is sure to be some other. With best insight, painstakingness, and expertise, Robbins takes us on a multi-faceted tour which ought to make all sensitive people query their nutritional styles maximum searchingly. I turned into not able to place it down."

Cleveland Amory author The Cat Who Came For Christmas

"Diet For a substitution America is famously discernible and sensible. Upheld with the aid of using massive examination, attractive, it directs the suitable reaction closer to the ugly troubles confronting humanity inner the approaching future. an excellent and thrilling paintings."

Helen Nearing author Living the incomparable Life

"Diet For a substitution America is probably a ground-breaking prosecution of our nutritional practices that ought to be perused with the aid of using every person interested by strong residing. it is an all-round explored, very an awful lot reported, and enlightening file of the fantasies and certainties approximately meat, milk, fat, and protein. I may have the choice to prescribe this ee-e book to sufferers, companions, and own circle of relatives members."

Dr. Andrew Weil author, Healthy Aging

"Diet For a substitution America is the first-rate ee-e book ever composed almost about making use of creatures for meals. I want I had composed it myself. I was in particular moved with the aid of using the way wherein Robbins exposed the difficulty with the aid of using expounding on creatures as residing, feeling, creatures."

Jim Mason author Animal Factories

"Diet For a substitution America is that the first-rate ee-e book I've perused withinside the maximum current ten years, probable ever. it is the top-ratede massive ee-e book of our age."

Dan Millman author The Way of The Peaceful Warrior.

* What Is Diet Culture American

If you've got got been following my weblog, you apprehend that I've mentioned "food plan lifestyle" in more than one weblog posts, which I formerly struggled with disordered ingesting - observed with the aid of using doing some inner home tasks and turning into a non-food plan dietitian and a fitness educate who specializes in Intuitive Eating and makes use of a Health at Every Size (HAES) perspective. you apprehend that I often point out why weight-reduction plan would not paintings for plenty human beings, and the manner that makes a speciality of our behaviors - as opposed to range on a scale - are frequently empowering for our well-being - and perhaps a very good manner to stay our progress.

So nowadays I'm switching gears and am offering a hint greater rationalization on what food plan lifestyle is, moreover to discussing a few samples of its have an effect on for the duration of a form of situation. Please recognise that it is absolutely comprehensible if - as you are analyzing this - you revel in extraordinary emotions. Some is probably sadness, frustration, anger, defensiveness, etc. We're beat this collectively! Unfortunately, beginning as children, our Western lifestyle has supplied us with many unflattering portrayals of large our bodies in cartoons, kid's books, films, etc. And those poor characterizations keep in the course of existence - which means that it is enormously probable which you without a doubt would possibly perceive with some of what is written for the duration of this publish. I'm satisfied to speak approximately any mind or emotions which might also additionally arise as you are analyzing this! I'm humbly penning this publish as a person who has skilled heaps of skinny privilege in the course of existence, and whose questioning keeps to conform due to my awesome customers and mentors who train me this kind of lot.

WHAT IS DIET CULTURE?

I'll proportion a hint of my interpretation of food plan lifestyle. Diet lifestyle can be a fixed of ideals revolving across the concept "thin" our bodies are the most suitable, valuable, and "healthy."

Diet lifestyle additionally conveys that ingesting a specific manner is "good" or "bad" - which an person's really well worth will increase while ingesting "healthy," or while residing for the duration of a small frame. It's really well worth noting that food plan lifestyle has often provided a photo of fitness as residing for the duration of an able-bodied, small, white frame. As Christy Harrison, MPH, RD, CDN, writes, "Diet lifestyle can be a form of oppression, and dismantling it is important for developing a international it really is simply and non violent for human beings altogether our bodies." If you would want to analyze greater approximately food plan lifestyle's records and form of oppression, listen Christy Harrison point out this difficulty for the duration of this podcast beginning spherical the twenty-two-minute mark.

Diet lifestyle's have an effect on can in reality be located in the food plan enterprise. While the food plan enterprise tells you that every one your desires will come real as soon as you acquire a bit frame and consume a specific manner, it would not let you know that weight-reduction plan would not upload the lengthy-time period for plenty human beings; are frequently dangerous emotionally, physically, and mentally; perhaps a robust hazard thing for growing an ingesting disorder; can be a robust predictor of weight gain; which weight cycling - that's associated with yo-yo weight-reduction plan - is related to worsened cardiovascular fitness and untimely death.

Among many matters, food plan lifestyle's have an effect on can purpose growing weight bias - which has negative mind approximately human beings way to their frame length or weight. Weight bias can then result in weight stigma - which involves setting labels on human beings way to their frame length and discriminating in opposition to them - which may be dangerous to the ones people' emotional, physical, and intellectual well-being. In reality, weight stigma is an unbiased hazard thing for persistent fitness conditions. Weight stigma can then purpose internalized weight stigma, for the duration of which an person starts to accept as true with that the labels which are thrown at them are real - which may be in particular adverse to the man or woman's typical fitness. Internalized weight stigma is associated with persistent weight-reduction plan, ingesting issues, reduced preference to workout, etc.

DIET CULTURE'S INFLUENCE are frequently FOUND IN MANY PLACES

I've indexed beneath only a few of the diverse locations in which food plan lifestyle's have an effect on is frequently located. As you'll see in some of the following examples, food plan lifestyle's have an effect on can purpose length discrimination:

Grocery shops:

An worker complimenting a consumer for being "so good," on the queue while figuring out that the customer is shopping for an oversized quantity of "healthy" ingredients.

A grocery consumer taking images of the meals in his or her cart - and posting it on Instagram with a "clean" ingesting message or "If I can roll withinside the hay, you may too" statement.

An person searching right into a grocery cart containing sweets, and questioning that the customer is being "bad" for getting the ones items.

Healthcare:

Health experts raising smaller our bodies - and making the concept that a smaller frame is "healthy" entirely way to its length - at the same time as viewing a larger frame as "unhealthy" entirely way to its length.

A affected person is available in with a damaged arm and is informed to lessen.

Not diagnosing or treating a circumstance way to being distracted with the aid of using an person's better weight - and entirely suggesting weight reduction. Also lacking a prognosis due to questioning that a thin-bodied man or woman is "healthy."

Health practitioners viewing sufferers in large our bodies as undisciplined and "noncompliant with treatment." some of the most disciplined folks who I do recognise are human beings in large our bodies.

Labeling a thin-bodied dietitian as "good," and a dietitian for the duration of a bigger frame as "bad." Spoil alert: There are severa ROCKSTAR dietitians in smaller and larger our bodies.

Not considering the effect that the discrimination that we might also additionally revel in because of our complexion, ethnicity, gender, sexual orientation, socioeconomic repute, and frame length can put on our fitness.

Not being conscious of ways an person's genetics, pressure levels, degree of self-care, and socioeconomic repute can have an effect on one's wellness.

Workplace:

I turned into simply getting ready to require an utter of a child carrot while a former coworker requested me, "Do you apprehend what number carbohydrates are in that?!" you would have notion I was approximately capable of consume some thing toxic! My reaction turned into, "Yes! and they're delicious!" You get the purpose. My carrot turned into being categorized as "bad" as it contained carbohydrates. i certainly like carbs, and respect that they're the gold trendy for offering us with energy!

It's felony to terminate an person's employment supported weight in forty nine states inside us. Here's a few greater records approximately length discrimination. Some studies additionally shows that better weight personnel have fewer process opportunities, and are paid much less in comparison to human beings in decrease weight our bodies -, in particular girls.

Weight loss demanding situations at paintings - which make stronger the notion that being smaller is suitable and healthier. albeit we are now no longer brooding approximately how this task makes a few better weight human beings FEEL (Receiving the message that there may be some thing incorrect with their our bodies, and hence there need to be a competition at paintings to restore them), it is really well worth noting that weight/frame length is often a inaccurate indicator of fitness. If businesses need to empower their personnel' fitness, it'd make greater feel to specialise in matters that make high-quality and sustainable change, like fitness-selling behaviors that sense proper to the workers - which might also additionally empower an person's fitness at ANY length.

it's also really well worth noting that the perceived weight stigma that better weight people revel in usually - which they are enduring for the duration of this paintings-associated instance with the aid of using the manner - "doubles the threat of excessive allostatic load." Allostatic load refers to physiological dysregulation in the frame, like lipid/metabolic, glucose metabolism, and inflammation. So in different words, weight reduction demanding situations might also additionally make contributions to harming an worker's well-being. Some studies in addition shows that decreasing weight stigma might also additionally empower a higher weight man or woman's fitness with the aid of using in reality lowering the physiological dysregulation in the man or woman's frame.

Gyms:

While there are a few gyms cropping up that sell a greater inclusive, frame-high-quality vibe, many gyms nonetheless raise smaller our bodies and consequently the concept of exercise to get a smaller frame.

There are tales of a few health teachers main a group elegance and speaking approximately "burning off" a specific meals with the aid of using doing that workout. This insinuates that we are able to now no longer eat meals and enjoy it, that it need to be "burned off" in order to own a bit frame,

and initiatives the notion that workout ought to be used for weight reduction - as opposed to for the intention of doing some thing that we enjoy, allows us sense well, and promotes coronary heart fitness.

The "clean" ingesting messages are plentiful, as are human beings being categorized or labeling themselves as "good" or "bad" - relying on whether or not or now no longer they made it to the gym.

Restaurants:

Clients have shared tales of strangers making feedback to them approximately what they are ingesting and consequently the amount of meals that they're consuming - which can be a end result of food plan lifestyle's have an effect on. This consists of being "good" and "bad" for ingesting positive meals and quantities of meals.

Some eating places do not provide chairs with out palms or an big sales space with a movable table, making it more difficult for human beings in large our bodies to in shape the chairs or booths. People of all sizes have the right to require up space.

TV, radio, films, books, and magazines:

The majority of the characters on TV and in films are thin-bodied - portraying smaller our bodies due to the fact the maximum suitable. regular with the National Eating Disorders Association (NEDA), "The first-rate-recognized environmental contributor to the occasion of ingesting issues is that the sociocultural idealization of thinness."

Many images of higher weight human beings are headless in information tales - that's dehumanizing.

There's an abundance of mag articles and books committed to the most recent decreasing food plan, "clean" ingesting, and hints for a manner to lessen.

From kid's cartoons to films in the course of our lifetime, human beings in large our bodies are portrayed as on the first-rate - stupid and funny - and on the worst, lazy, sloppy, etc.

Social media accounts:

There's a tremendous quantity of "clean" ingesting accounts, health posts revolving across the intention of being thin-bodied, demonizing a variety of meals, the advertising of diverse diets, etc.

Bullying human beings in large our bodies take region regularly - which includes threats of violence.

Clothing shops:

While the quantity of plus-length garments stores and fashion-ahead alternatives is increasing, there may be such plenty of room for improvement.

Around 67% of americanee girls are plus-length, sporting length 14 or better - and but severa shops fail to deliver many alternatives for smaller and larger our bodies.

Being charged more money for plus-length garb.

human beings that put on a length eleven shoe are charged an equal amount of money as human beings that put on a length 6 shoe. collectively designer states, "We not often see tall and maternity versions of garb being priced differently. It's merciless and unfair to unmarried out one somatotype ."

This listing is going on and on. Now which you've were given examine this listing, it are frequently useful to music into how and while food plan lifestyle is influencing our questioning. this could assist us keep away from discriminating in opposition to others - and assist enhance our attitudes in the direction of ourselves additionally . the first-rate information is that once all of us recognise greater, we are able to do higher.

we might want to parent on lessening food plan lifestyle's have an effect on, and selling equality for ALL our bodies.

In an upcoming article, i may be capable of endorse more than one moves which you without a doubt can fancy reduce the effect that food plan lifestyle has in your very own existence. Until then, I invite all parents to task our questioning, and consequently the taking into consideration others - just so we are able to lessen food plan lifestyle's have an effect on on our society.

SARA JACKLINE

www.ingramcontent.com/pod-product-compliance
Lightning Source LLC
LaVergne TN
LVHW060832170826
845678LV00010B/1961
9798846368910